PERFECTLY QUEER

of related interest

In Their Shoes
Navigating Non-Binary Life
Jamie Windust
ISBN 978 1 78775 242 9
eISBN 978 1 78775 243 6

How to Be Ace
A Memoir of Growing Up Asexual
Rebecca Burgess
ISBN 978 1 78775 215 3
eISBN 978 1 78775 216 0

The Book of Non-Binary Joy
Ben Pechey
Illustrated by Sam Prentice
ISBN 978 1 78775 910 7
eISBN 978 1 78775 911 4

Queerly Autistic
The Ultimate Guide for LGBTQIA+ Teens on the Spectrum
Erin Ekins
ISBN 978 1 78775 171 2
eISBN 978 1 78775 172 9

An Illustrated Introduction

Victoria Barron

Jessica Kingsley Publishers
London and Philadelphia

First published in Great Britain in 2023 by Jessica Kingsley Publishers
An imprint of Hodder & Stoughton Ltd
An Hachette Company

1

A CIP catalogue record for this title is available from the British Library
and the Library of Congress

ISBN 978 1 83997 408 3
eISBN 978 1 83997 409 0

Printed and bound in China by Leo Paper Products Limited

Jessica Kingsley Publishers' policy is to use papers that are
natural, renewable, and recyclable products and made from wood
grown in sustainable forests. The logging and manufacturing
processes are expected to conform to the environmental
regulations of the country of origin.

Jessica Kingsley Publishers
Carmelite House
50 Victoria Embankment
London EC4Y 0DZ

www.jkp.com

CONTENTS

ABOUT THE AUTHOR

Victoria (she/her) is an illustrator who identifies with a variety of LGBTQ+ labels, and is a self-proclaimed 'queer weirdo' (...or would that be 'q-weirdo'?). She enjoys creating works that make people smile, often applying a fun twist to themes of self-worth, acceptance, or awareness and education.

Many of her works can be found via her Instagram account, @victoriabarronart, or website, www.victoriabarron.com.

ABOUT THE BOOK

Let's face it: learning about the countless LGBTQ+ topics and definitions can feel a little bit daunting. With a tendency to get easily overwhelmed or distracted, Victoria (on her own identity journey) found a frustrating lack of easy-to-understand LGBTQ+ information available from any one source.

So, she scoured resources from LGBTQ+-supporting charities and organisations, dove into various groups and blog posts, and spoke to people from across communities to better understand the diversity of queer experiences.

Continuing to explore and expand her understanding, Victoria began spreading some of this information online to make LGBTQ+ education easier for others in similar situations.

The project grew; she began assembling her art alongside manageable nuggets of queer-based information, dividing this with 'breathing space' activity pages featuring her 'pun-ny' rainbow mascot—The Rain-boa Constrictor.

The Rain-boa
Constrictor

And so, this book was born!

It covers everything from gender identity, assigned sex, sexual and romantic orientations to terminology, the acronym, common queer-ies, and more! For allies and queer folks alike, delve a little further into the wonderful aspects that create and surround the LGBTQ+ community in this (hopefully) perfectly queer introduction!

Disclaimer

LGBTQ+ flags, terms, and definitions may change/evolve over time, and no offence or confusion is intended should any such changes conflict with the contents of this publication. All information was deemed correct at the time of design, with terms and identities combining a variety of factors (including the voices of LGBTQ+ communities, dictionary descriptions, and a personal interpretation/ understanding) to create their definitions.

Even those within the community can—*and do*—make mistakes while navigating the many terms and nuanced definitions that continue to evolve. And you, lovely reader, might also make a few along the way... and that's OK. Confusion and slip-ups are a common part of the learning process, which is why it's important to allow yourself (and others) the space to grow with support and forgiveness.

INTRODUCTION

Useful terminology

Understanding some of these often-used LGBTQ+ terms may help with the definitions covered within—and beyond—this book.

Acespec/ace   Acespec is a shortened term for 'asexual spectrum' (referring to the spectrum *itself*), while 'ace' is commonly used to identify a person as being *on* the asexual spectrum (e.g. *They are ace, I am ace*).

AFAB   Assigned female at birth (used in relation to ASAB; see below).

AGAB   Assigned/assumed gender at birth. Refers to the assumed gender identity (e.g. boy/man or girl/woman) an individual will have based on their assigned sex at birth.

Allocishet   This term combines *allo*-sexual/romantic, *cis*gender, and *hetero*-sexual/*hetero*romantic. A person who is allocishet (and not intersex) isn't considered part of the LGBTQ+ community because all parts of their orientation, gender identity, and assigned sex are considered non-queer.

Alloromantic   A person who distinctly *and* consistently experiences romantic attraction. The opposite of aromantic.

Allosexual A person who distinctly *and* consistently experiences sexual attraction. The opposite of asexual.

AMAB Assigned male at birth (used in relation to ASAB; see below).

Amatonormativity The societal assumption that every individual should desire/follow traditional relationship constructs and expectations, such as wanting a marital status, children, sexual/romantic relationships, or monogamous relationships.

Arospec/aro Arospec is a shortened term for 'aromantic spectrum' (referring to the spectrum *itself*), while 'aro' (pronounced as either 'arrow' or 'aye-row') is commonly used to identify a person as being *on* the aromantic spectrum (e.g. *They are aro, I am aro*).

ASAB Assigned sex at birth. The biological classification of male, female, or (the many variations of) intersex, assigned at birth.

ASAB might be a preferred term for some people since 'biological sex' may feel inaccurate or insensitive.

Inaccurate/insensitive example: *They are a trans man, but they are biologically female.*

Preferred example: *They were assigned female at birth, but they are a trans man.*

Attraction Attraction is an instinctive interest experienced by an individual. It is innate and cannot be forcibly directed OR chosen.

Binary gender A way to describe gender that's distinctly experienced as (the traditional construct of) either 'boy/man' or 'girl/woman'.

Binary sex A way to describe an individual's biological sex (ASAB; see above) being classified as either traditionally 'male' or 'female'.

Cisnormative   The idea that every individual will identify with the gender assigned to them at birth, and any experience outside of this (e.g. transgender) is not considered.

Cis/cisgender   A term to describe people whose experience of gender is the same as that assigned/assumed at birth. The opposite of 'trans'.

Dyadic   Dyadic can be used to describe a person born with characteristics that clearly adhere to the traditional (binary sex) classifications of male or female.

Heteronormative   The idea that every individual will experience hetero-sexual/romantic attraction by default.

Identity   An LGBTQ+ identity label relates to an individual's experience of gender (as in: *My gender identity is fluid*) and/or an individual's sexual and romantic orientation (as in: *I identify as asexual and panromantic*).

Man-aligned and **woman-aligned**   Umbrella terms for some non-binary people to distinguish their experience of gender as often/ significantly/partially—*but not entirely*—aligned with the traditional construct of 'binary man' or 'binary woman' (demiboy, demigirl, etc.).

Mono-sexual/romantic   Describes sexual and/or romantic attraction for a singular gender. Hetero-sexual/romantic or homo-sexual/ romantic orientations are usually considered as falling under the mono-sexual/romantic spectrum.

Mspec   A shortened term for the multi-sexual/romantic spectrum. Orientations that experience attraction to multiple genders fall under the multi-sexual/romantic spectrum.

Non-binary genders   A way to describe genders that are not solely/completely either 'binary man' or 'binary woman'. Non-binary identities may be fluid, changeable, or fixed within the vast spectrum of gender, and thus (depending on the individual) may be described as both a gender or a gender identity.

Orientation   A term used to describe how an individual is sexually and/or romantically aligned. This can be broken down into two key components: 1) What gender(s) an individual is sexually and/or romantically attracted to, and 2) How sexual and/or romantic attraction is experienced by an individual (on the spectrum between a-sexual/romantic and allo-sexual/romantic).

Perioriented   A term describing aligned sexual and romantic orientations—the 'who attraction is felt towards', or the 'how the attraction is experienced', will match for both orientations.

Usually (with a few ace/aro exceptions), a perioriented individual will have matching prefixes (e.g. *pan*sexual and *pan*romantic), but because matching attractions are the predominant/assumed experience, one can simply use the suffix 'sexual' to inform their alignment.

Pronouns   Identifiers that refer to a singular person, or multiple people, in place of their name. Pronouns are generally any combination of she/her/hers (singular use), he/him/his (singular use), or they/them/theirs (singular and multiple use).

The gender spectrum   The concept that gender resides on a spectrum encompassing binary gender (man/woman) along with the many and variable non-binary/genderless identities.

The spectrum of sex   The concept that biological classifications of sex can reside on a spectrum to encompass binary sex (male/female) as well as the wide range of intersex classifications.

Trans/transgender   A term for people whose inner experience of gender is different to the gender assigned/assumed at birth. The opposite of 'cis'.

Trans binary   Applies to trans men and trans women who *don't* feel a connection with their assigned gender at birth (the 'trans' part), but *do* feel a connection with the binary construct of 'man' or 'woman' (the 'binary' part).

Trans non-binary   Applies to trans people who *don't* feel a connection with their assigned gender at birth (the 'trans' part), and *also* feel a partial/changeable/lack of connection with the binary constructs of 'man' or 'woman' (the 'non-binary' part).

Umbrella term   A broad term to encompass many variations/ elements and identities within it. An umbrella term is connected yet separate from an identity of the same name. A few common LGBTQ+ examples are:

- 'Queer' (an individual identity label) and 'the queer umbrella' (a broad term).
- 'Non-binary' (an individual identity label) and 'the non-binary umbrella' (a broad term).
- 'Trans' (an individual identity label) and 'the trans umbrella' (a broad term).

Varioriented   A term describing non-aligned sexual and romantic orientations—the 'who attraction is felt towards', or the 'how the attraction is experienced', does not match for both orientations.

Varioriented individuals often (but not exclusively) reside on the asexual and/or aromantic spectrums, but can reside entirely on the allo-sexual/romantic end of the spectrum. The prefixes used for both orientations will not usually match; such as: *a*sexual and *pan*romantic, *bi*sexual and *a*romantic, *homo*sexual (gay/lesbian) and *omni*romantic.*

*Refer to the 'Pride Flags' section for helpful identity definitions.

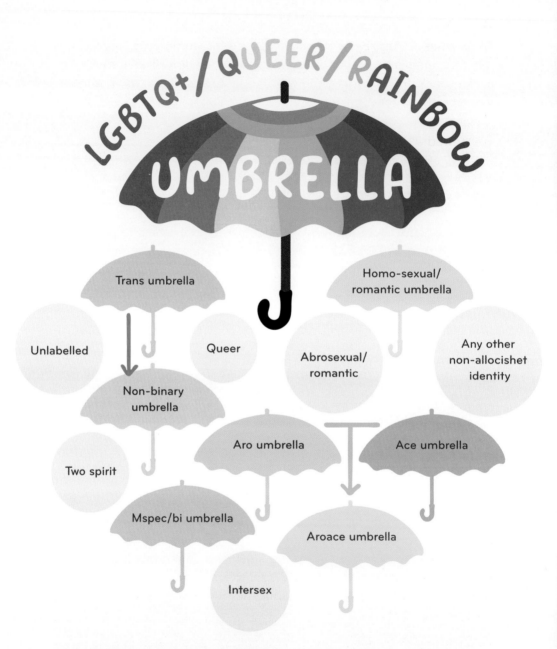

LGBTQ+/QUEER/RAINBOW

UMBRELLA

Trans umbrella

Homo-sexual/ romantic umbrella

Unlabelled

Queer

Abrosexual/ romantic

Any other non-allocishet identity

Non-binary umbrella

Two spirit

Aro umbrella

Ace umbrella

Mspec/bi umbrella

Aroace umbrella

Intersex

The LGBTQ+ umbrella (also called the queer/rainbow umbrella) is the metaphorical umbrella under which any LGBTQ+ identity resides. These identities, in turn, can branch out to include numerous other umbrellas beneath them, and so on.

Types of relationship

Though partnered relationships beyond amatonormative expectations might be considered queer, there is debate for their inclusion under the LGBTQ+ acronym. This is because relationships are viewed as an active choice—unlike gender identity, assigned sex at birth, or sexual/romantic orientation (which are all things innate to the individual).

Defining a type of partnered relationship as queer can often depend on the individuals involved, since participants might be either allocishet or part of the LGBTQ+ community. There is, however, better representation for certain types of partnered relationships (such as polyamory) under the GSRM (gender, sexual, and romantic minorities) acronym—an alternate/sister acronym to 'LGBTQ+'.

Diamoric relationship

In addition to being an identity and umbrella term, 'diamoric' can be used to describe a relationship in which at least one person is non-binary. A diamoric relationship can be a useful definition when describing it, as 'straight/hetero relationship' might otherwise not feel comfortable for any person involved.

A person whose gender is binary (man or woman) cannot use the term as an identity, only to describe their relationship with a non-binary partner.

Monogamy

The most socially expected (amatonormative) type of partnered relationship, monogamy refers to a state between two individuals in which both parties regard their relationship as closed (non-polyamorous) and exclusive to each other.

Monogamous relationships can include solely queer or non-queer individuals, or a combination of both.

Polyamory

A type of relationship between multiple individuals that might include a relationship between a specific group of partners, or an individual who has multiple relationships that are separate from each other. All parties within a polyamorous relationship are aware of, and consenting to, each individual involved.

Polyamorous relationships can include solely queer or non-queer individuals, or a combination of both.

Polyplatonic relationship

A non-monogamous version of a QPR, with all parties aware of, and consenting to, each individual involved. Similar to polyamory, a polyplatonic relationship can be between a specific group of partners, or an individual who has multiple relationships that are separate from each other.

Polyplatonic relationships (like QPRs) may be more likely for aromantic or arospec people, but are not exclusive to those in the queer community.

Queerplatonic relationship

Queerplatonic relationships are also called QPRs. The term refers to a monogamous partnership between individuals who experience a deep emotional bond (e.g. platonic love) but who do not experience romantic attraction for each other. This can also be thought of as a committed platonic partnership and may involve commitments such as living together, buying a house together, marriage, or children.

QPRs may be more likely for aromantic or arospec people, but are not exclusive to those in the queer community.

Soft romo

A type of relationship (monogamous or non-monogamous) with low-level romance. This can be useful for individuals who experience partial, ambiguous, or changing levels of romantic attraction (such as arospec people), but also for those who simply dislike (or feel uncomfortable with) relationships that have overly romance-coded elements/expectations/actions.

Criss-crosss...

Across

1 Assigned gender at birth (abbreviation).
2 Descriptor for one's sense of self.
3 Identifiers for singular and/or multiple people.
4 Descriptor for how one defines their sexual/romantic identity.
5 Part of an umbrella term that can describe a person whose gender is often/significantly/partially experienced as 'man' or 'woman'.
6 Not identifying with the gender that's assigned at birth (shortened term).
7 Biological classification (e.g. male or female).
8 Assigned female at birth (abbreviation).

Down

9 Used to define an innate appeal.
10 Assigned male at birth (abbreviation).
11 Term for a person who is allo-sexual/romantic, and cisgender, and hetero-sexual/romantic.
12 Not identifying completely with binary 'man' or 'woman'.
13 Assigned sex at birth (abbreviation).
14 Social/cultural construct (e.g. 'man' or 'woman').
15 Identifying with the gender that's assigned at birth (shortened term).

DEFINING ORIENTATION

Understanding types of attraction

Since sexual and romantic attraction (*how* it's experienced, and to *whom*) are what define an individual's sexual/romantic orientation it can be helpful to distinguish the differences between common forms of attraction.

Any form of attraction may be experienced separately or simultaneously with others, and its inherent nature means it cannot be chosen or directed. It's also important to recognise that deep affection and/or a sense of intimacy are not exclusive to any one form of attraction, and none should be viewed as having more 'value' than the next.

Sexual attraction

Feeling an innate desire to engage in sexual activity with someone. Sexual attraction is often confused with libido/arousal; while sexual attraction has a specific direction—it is specifically directed towards someone— libido/arousal is a purely physical need for sexual release and not specifically directed towards anyone.

Romantic attraction

This can be difficult to define since the idea and experience of romantic attraction can vary from person to person. It is commonly described as feeling a desire to be romantic with someone, adhering to the traditional concept of romance, romantic actions, or romantic feelings.

Sensual attraction

Describes a desire for physical touch with someone. This can be for a sense of comfort, intimacy, or pleasure, and may include things like hugging, kissing, massage, holding hands, etc. Sensual attraction can be either sexual or non-sexual in nature.

Aesthetic attraction

Being drawn to the appearance/style of someone and finding them pleasing to look at (in a similar way that one can appreciate a beautiful view).

Physical attraction

Finding a particular physique pleasing to look at and/or being drawn to a particular physical build or aspects of someone.

Emotional attraction

Being drawn to *who someone is as a person*; desiring a bond because of an individual's true personality. This desire for emotional connection can be, for example, familial, parental, platonic, romantic, or alterous (see below) in nature.

Intellectual attraction

Being drawn to—or desiring a connection with—an individual based on their intellectual mind/ability.

Platonic attraction

Desiring an affectionate and meaningful bond with someone in which romantic attraction does not play a part.

Alterous attraction

An experience that resides somewhere within the nebulous area between platonic and romantic attraction—not considered specifically romantic or specifically platonic. Sometimes experienced by (but not limited to) some arospec identities.

The split-attraction model

The split-attraction model (sometimes shortened to the acronym SAM) is used to illustrate how a person's sexual attraction and romantic attraction do not mirror each other. This is helpful for varioriented people, including the majority of acespec and/or arospec identities.

NOTE: Please refer to the descriptions within the Pride Flags section for a better understanding of each aspec and ace orientation.

We can use the examples on both diagrams to demonstrate how a person's sexual and romantic orientations are unaligned.

Examples

✔ **Person A:** Sexual orientation = greysexual lesbian
Romantic orientation = aromantic

O **Person B:** Sexual orientation = asexual
Romantic orientation = heteroromantic

✗ **Person C:** Sexual orientation = demi polysexual
Romantic orientation = pan greyromantic

SEXUALITY

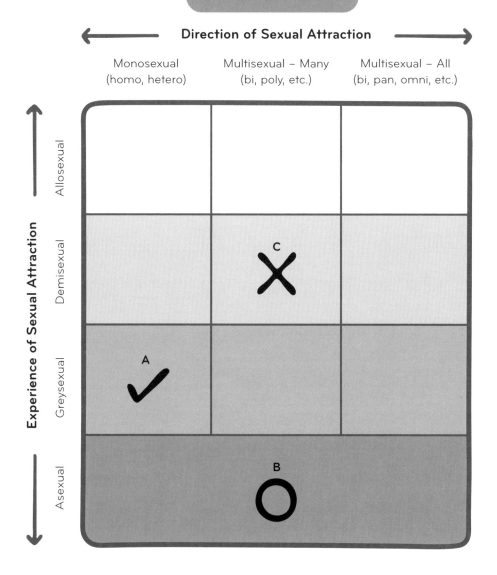

Direction of Sexual Attraction

Monosexual (homo, hetero)   Multisexual – Many (bi, poly, etc.)   Multisexual – All (bi, pan, omni, etc.)

Experience of Sexual Attraction

Allosexual

Demisexual — C ✗

Greysexual — A ✓

Asexual — B ◯

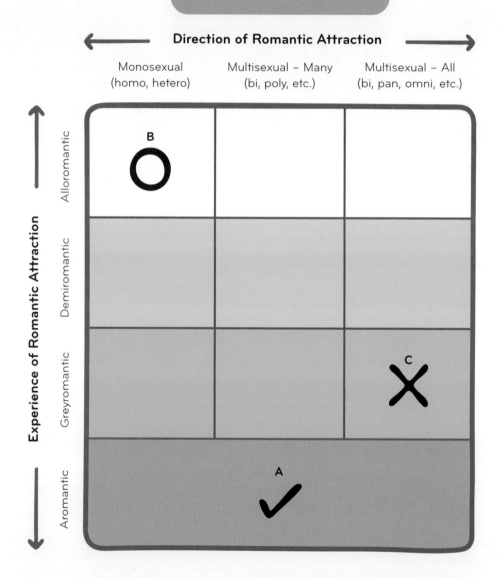

The aro and ace umbrellas

The aro umbrella

This is the metaphorical umbrella containing all arospec identities, with many further labels or micro-labels found beneath its greyromantic umbrella.

The ace umbrella

This is the metaphorical umbrella containing all acespec identities, with many further labels or micro-labels found beneath its greysexual umbrella.

The aroace umbrella

This is connected to the aro and ace umbrellas, combining identities from both to create its own unique experience.

(Also referred to as the aromantic spectrum)   (Also referred to as the asexual spectrum)

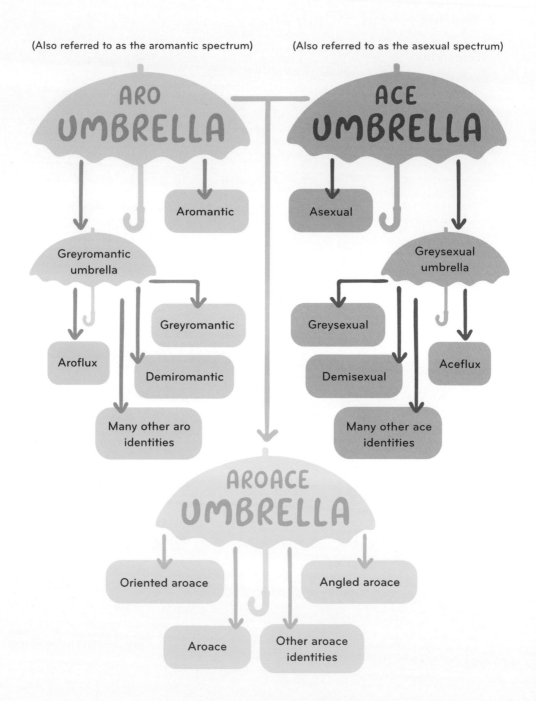

The mspec/bi umbrella

Depending on personal preference, this umbrella can be called either the mspec umbrella, the multi-sexual/romantic umbrella, or the bi umbrella. It contains any multi-sexual/romantic orientations, covering attraction that's experienced towards some/many/all/any genders.

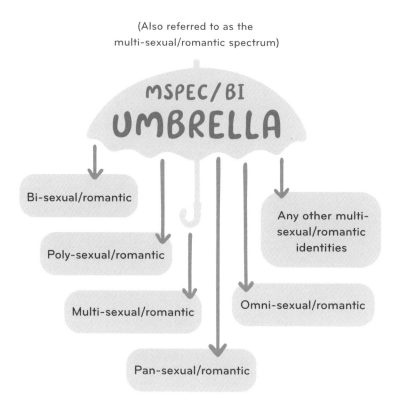

(Also referred to as the
multi-sexual/romantic spectrum)

MSPEC/BI
UMBRELLA

Bi-sexual/romantic

Poly-sexual/romantic

Multi-sexual/romantic

Pan-sexual/romantic

Omni-sexual/romantic

Any other multi-sexual/romantic identities

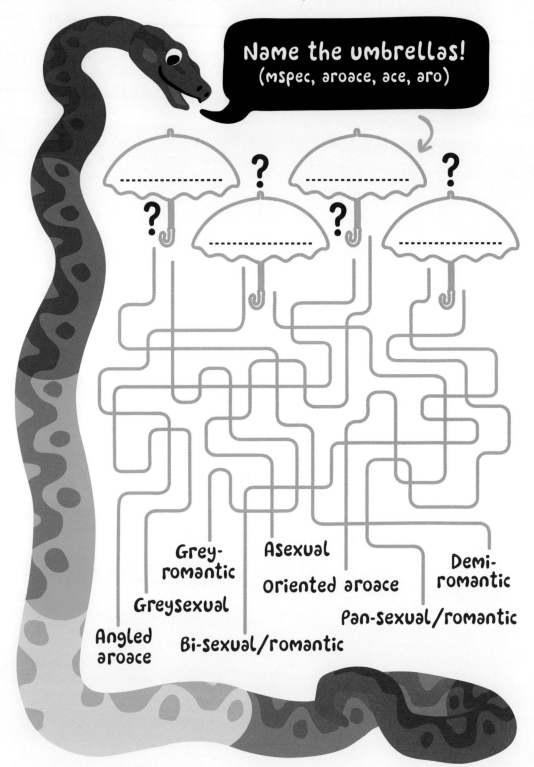

Name the umbrellas!
(mspec, aroace, ace, aro)

SEX & GENDER

The spectrum of sex

Biological sex can be better understood when viewed as a spectrum: male and female, and the many, diverse intersex classifications between these.

In 1993, Dr Anne Fausto-Sterling proposed five ways biological sex might be categorised beyond the mainstream binary view: female, male, hermaphrodite, female pseudohermaphrodite, and male pseudohermaphrodite. She expanded the idea of biological sex as a spectrum in her 2000 article, 'The Five Sexes Revisited', so as to not be defined by a set/limited number of classifications; rather, 'sex and gender are best conceptualised as points in a multidimensional space.'[1]

BIOLOGICAL SEX

FEMALE
Assigned female at birth (AFAB)

INTERSEX
The many variations between female and male

MALE
Assigned male at birth (AMAB)

---

1 Fausto-Sterling, A. (2000) 'The Five Sexes Revisited.' *The Sciences*, July/August, p.22.

Gender

Gender is a social construct in which 'man' is often associated with being male/masculine, and 'woman' is often associated with being female/feminine. When discussing the broader topic of gender, it can be thought of as a complex mix of these traditional expectations along with one's own sense of identity and the choices made to reflect that (gender expression/presentation and behaviours).

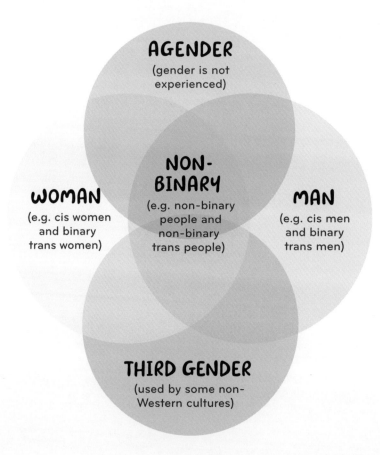

AGENDER
(gender is not experienced)

NON-BINARY
(e.g. non-binary people and non-binary trans people)

WOMAN
(e.g. cis women and binary trans women)

MAN
(e.g. cis men and binary trans men)

THIRD GENDER
(used by some non-Western cultures)

The experience of gender

GENDER IDENTITY

How gender is experienced by the inner self; determined by the individual.

GENDER EXPRESSION

How gender can be expressed, presented, or communicated (such as appearance/style mannerisms, behaviour, gender roles, etc.).

FEMININE

Traditionally perceived feminine traits/ behaviours and/or characteristics.

MASCULINE

Traditionally perceived masculine traits/ behaviours and/or characteristics.

ANDROGYNOUS

Neither overtly feminine or masculine, but a combination/ blend of both qualities.

NEUTRAL

Not displaying qualities that are either feminine or masculine.

BIOLOGICAL SEX

Biological anatomy, chromosomes, and hormones. Also referred to as assigned sex at birth (ASAB).

Pronouns

Though the pronouns of others are often presumed (often based on a person's gender presentation/expression), they may not be correct/respectful for that individual—this is why confirmation of one's pronouns is always preferable.

Feminine, masculine, or neutral pronouns can be used in many combinations regardless of gender, and may be fixed, flexible, or ever-changing. For example: a woman might consistently use she/her pronouns, while a demiboy individual might use he/him and sometimes they/them pronouns, and a genderfluid individual might change regularly between he/she/they (depending on their current gender experience).

SHE/HER/HERS

'Feminine'-associated pronouns (she/her/hers) are often assumed for a perceived/presenting woman.

HE/HIM/HIS

'Masculine'-associated pronouns (he/him/his) are often assumed for a perceived/presenting man.

THEY/THEM/THEIRS

They/them/theirs are referred to as 'neutral' pronouns (since they have neither feminine or masculine associations), and as such, can be applied regardless of a person's binary or non-binary gender. They/them are often used to describe multiple individuals...*but*, they can also be used within a singular context, such as:

- When **a** person specifically identifies **their** pronouns as such.

- When **a** person's gender is currently unknown.

- When **a** person (whether their gender is known or not) is being written in a third-person perspective.

SHE/THEY   HE/THEY

SHE/HER   HE/HIM   THEY/THEM

SHE/HE   HE/SHE/THEY

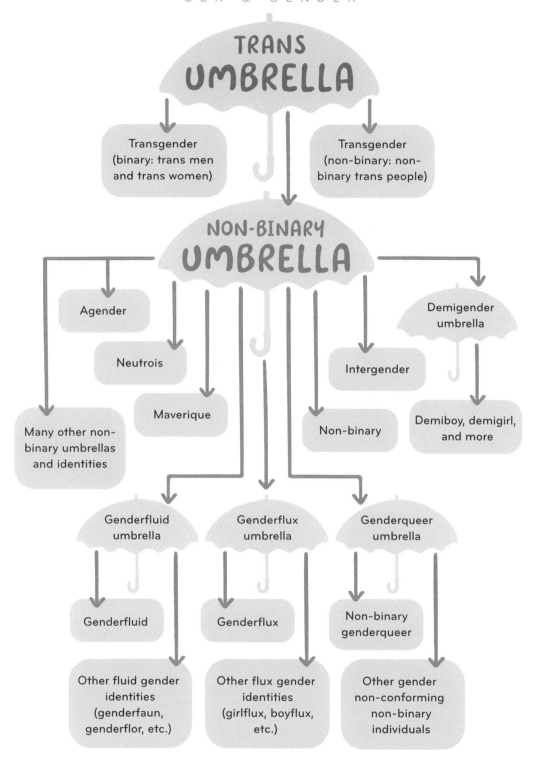

A: 01000001	H: 01001000	O: 01001111	V: 01010110
B: 01000010	I: 01001001	P: 01010000	W: 01010111
C: 01000011	J: 01001010	Q: 01010001	X: 01011000
D: 01000100	K: 01001011	R: 01010010	Y: 01011001
E: 01000101	L: 01001100	S: 01010011	Z: 01011010
F: 01000110	M: 01001101	T: 01010100	- : 00101101
G: 01000111	N: 01001110	U: 01010101	SPACE: 00100000

```
01010100 01001000 01000101 00100000
01010111 01001111 01010010 01001100
01000100 00100000 01001001 01010011
00100000 01000110 01010101 01001100
01001100 00100000 01001111 01000110
00100000 01000111 01000101 01001110
01000100 01000101 01010010 00101101
01010110 01000101 01010010 01010011
01001001 01010100 01011001
```

Binary Code Message

THE ACRONYM

Part of the alphabet mafia? In the alphabet soup? However it's referred to, the LGBTQ+ acronym works as an umbrella, housing all the queer identities and communities beneath it. The most recognised LGBT acronym (lesbian, gay, bisexual, transgender) has expanded over the years in an effort to be more inclusive...though there's no official order of letters for the extended acronym, as this can vary from country to country. The general consensus is that as long as the '+' is added, this will represent any of the additional identities.

Some possible acronym combinations you might see are:

- **LGBT+** (lesbian, gay, bisexual, transgender, +)
- **LGBTQ+** (lesbian, gay, bisexual, transgender, queer/ questioning, +)
- **LGBTQIA+** (lesbian, gay, bisexual, transgender, queer/ questioning, intersex, ace/aro/agender, +)
- **LGBTQ2S+** (lesbian, gay, bisexual, transgender, queer/ questioning, two spirit, +)
- **LGBTQ2IA+** (lesbian, gay, bisexual, transgender, queer/ questioning, two spirit, intersex, ace/aro/agender, +)

LGBTQIA+

The 'L' represents: LESBIAN

This may also represent any identity defined as women loving women (WLW), or non-men loving non-men.

ADD SOME COLOUR!

LES-BEE-AN

LGBTQIA+

The 'G' represents: GAY
This may also represent any identity defined as men loving men (MLM), or non-women loving non-women.

ADD SOME COLOUR!

GAY-ETY

LGBTQIA+

ADD SOME COLOUR!

The 'B' represents: BI-SEXUAL/ROMANTIC

Representing not only bi-sexual/romantic (the identity), but all multi-sexual/romantic identities under the mspec/bi umbrella.

LGBTQIA+

The 'T' represents: TRANSGENDER

Representing not only transgender (the identity), but all identities under the trans and non-binary umbrellas.

ADD SOME COLOUR!

TRANS-
PORT

LGBTQIA+

ADD SOME COLOUR!

The 'Q' represents: QUEER

Representing queer (the identity), and those who currently identify as 'questioning'.

QUEER-Y...

LGBTQIA+

The 'I' represents: INTERSEX

Representing intersex people (not relating to gender identity or sexual or romantic orientation, but a classification of sex).

ADD SOME COLOUR!

INN-TERSEX

LGBTQIA+

The 'A' represents: ACESPEC, AROSPEC, AGENDER

Representing identities with an 'A' prefix, such as asexual (and ace identities), aromantic (and aro identities), and agender.

ADD SOME COLOUR!

LGBTQIA+

The '+' represents: THE EXTENDED COMMUNITY
An important addition, representing any queer identity without
a designated letter (or not mentioned) in the acronym.

ADD SOME
COLOUR!

PLUS-HY

word sssearch!

N	U	G	A	Y	K	I	H	R	E	P	L	P	A	N
E	A	I	B	S	X	A	R	O	M	A	N	T	I	C
Q	L	N	R	E	Y	G	E	I	A	N	B	R	L	E
E	U	I	O	L	G	E	L	N	O	S	T	A	N	Q
I	A	E	S	D	I	N	U	A	B	E	U	D	U	N
N	X	R	E	N	B	D	Q	I	R	X	L	E	R	L
T	E	D	X	R	N	E	L	B	E	U	R	N	E	A
E	S	N	U	O	E	R	N	S	N	A	P	G	S	U
R	O	E	A	T	Y	B	I	E	X	L	R	E	N	X
S	M	G	L	E	I	N	A	L	R	E	X	O	L	E
E	N	E	X	I	M	C	N	O	D	U	A	R	B	S
X	I	U	N	O	N	B	I	N	A	R	Y	B	I	Y
N	B	I	S	E	X	U	A	L	T	U	M	A	N	L
A	S	E	A	C	I	T	N	M	O	R	A	E	A	O
P	N	T	R	A	N	S	G	E	N	D	E	R	U	P

LESBIAN   PANSEXUAL   ASEXUAL
GAY   TRANSGENDER   AROMANTIC
BISEXUAL   NON-BINARY   ABROSEXUAL
POLYSEXUAL   QUEER   AGENDER
OMNISEXUAL   INTERSEX

PRIDE FLAGS

When defining orientations, sources may cite 'sex' or 'gender' to describe the type or quantity of people that attraction is experienced to. This is where things can get complicated; you cannot know an individual's assigned sex or gender unless expressly informed by said individual. Sexual/romantic attraction might initially be determined (among other things) by *our assumption* of an individual's assigned sex (male, female, or an intersex classification) and/or *our perception* of an individual's gender expression/presentation (masculine, feminine, androgynous, neutral).

In the context of explaining orientations, the following definitions here shall be using the term 'gender' to represent the vast and complex classifiers of sexual/romantic attraction.

Key
(to show what aspect can contribute to forming an orientation/identity)

■ = Sexual attraction

♥ = Romantic attraction

● = Gender identity

■ ♥ = Sexual attraction OR sexual AND romantic attraction

■ ♥ ● = Sexual attraction AND/OR romantic attraction AND/OR gender identity

PRIDE FLAGS

LESBIAN 🏳️‍🌈💜
HOMOROMANTIC 💜

Women and woman-aligned people who are attracted to other women and woman-aligned people.

Also described as women loving women and non-men loving non-men.

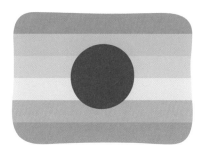

NEPTUNIC 🏳️‍🌈💜

Commonly used by women and non-binary people to describe an attraction towards women and (woman-aligned, feminine-aligned) non-binary people who are specifically not men, man-aligned, and masculine-aligned.

SAPPHIC 🏳️‍🌈💜

Describes women and woman-aligned people who experience attraction to (or have a pref-erence for) women and woman-aligned people.

Sapphic includes *exclusive* attraction (to only women/woman-aligned people), as well as *non-exclusive* attraction (to multiple genders).

TRIXIC 🏳️‍🌈💜

Defined as non-binary loving women (NBLW). Used specifically by non-binary people who experience attraction to (or have a preference for) women/woman-aligned people.

People using this label may also experience attraction to multiple genders.

PRIDE FLAGS

GAY/VINCIAN ■♥
HOMOROMANTIC ♥

Men and man-aligned people who are attracted to other men and man-aligned people. Also described as men loving men, and non-women loving non-women.

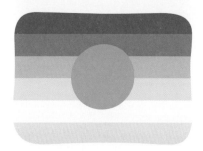

URANIC ■♥

Commonly used by men and non-binary people to describe an attraction towards men and (man-aligned, masculine-aligned, etc.) non-binary people who are specifically not women, woman-aligned, and feminine-aligned.

ACHILLEAN ■♥

Describes men and man-aligned people who experience attraction to (or have a preference for) other men/man-aligned people.

'Achillean' includes *exclusive* attraction (to only men/man-aligned people), as well as *non-exclusive* attraction (to multiple genders).

TORIC ■♥

Defined as non-binary loving men (NBLM). Used specifically by non-binary people who feel attraction to (or have a preference for) men/man-aligned people.

People using this label may also experience attraction to multiple genders.

PRIDE FLAGS

MULTISEXUAL ◻♥
MULTIROMANTIC ♥

A broad umbrella term for people who experience attraction to multiple genders (mspec orientations), it can also be used as an identity label to communicate an attraction to multiple genders, without having to specify a particular mspec identity.

SATURNIC ◻♥

Commonly used by non-binary people to describe an attraction to non-binary people who are androgynous in nature (androgynous-aligned).

ENBIAN ◻♥

Describes non-binary people who feel attraction to (or have a preference for) other non-binary people. It can be used by people who experience attraction to multiple genders (including binary or non-binary).

DIAMORIC ◻♥

As an identity label, diamoric is used by non-binary people to describe any (romantic and/or sexual) attraction that cannot be easily defined in terms of attraction to 'same', 'similar', 'opposite', or 'different' genders (due to their personal experience of non-binary gender).

59

BISEXUAL 🟦♥
BIROMANTIC ♥

An orientation in which attraction is experienced to multiple genders; the bi label *can* include attraction to all genders...*but* it doesn't always have to. For example: while one bi person might experience attraction to many genders, another might experience attraction to all genders.

Though the prefix ('bi') means 'two', its use can represent an attraction towards 'two or more' genders, and/or to recognise a dual aspect of attraction: attraction to the 'same/similar' genders and to 'other/different' genders.

POLYSEXUAL 🟦♥
POLYROMANTIC ♥

A poly-sexual/romantic person specifically experiences attraction towards many genders... *but* not to all genders (e.g. attraction to men and to any non-binary identities, but not to women).

The prefix, 'poly', comes from Greek, meaning 'many'.

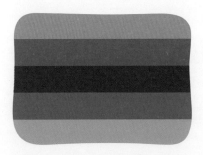

OMNISEXUAL 🟦♥
OMNIROMANTIC ♥

Attraction is specifically experienced towards all genders; however, the gender of a person can play a significant role in an omni-sexual/romantic person's attraction.

The prefix, 'omni', comes from Latin, meaning 'all'.

PRIDE FLAGS

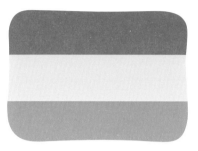

PANSEXUAL 🔲🩶 ♥
PANROMANTIC ♥

Attraction is specifically experienced towards all genders, with the gender of others not playing a significant role in a pan-sexual/romantic person's attraction.

The prefix, 'pan', comes from Greek, meaning 'all'.

ACESPEC 🔲

The acespec flag was created to represent all identities on the asexual spectrum. However, it's still common to see the asexual flag (black, grey, white, purple) representing not only the individual asexual identity but also the entire asexual spectrum.

ASEXUAL 🔲

An orientation in which a person specifically experiences no sexual attraction. Beyond their orientation, an asexual person may experience other forms of attraction (aesthetic, romantic, etc.) and can also have any level of libido.

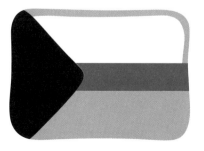

DEMISEXUAL 🔲

An acespec identity in which sexual attraction may occur only after a strong emotional bond has formed. However, there is no time frame in which, or guarantee that, this could happen with each partner.

PRIDE FLAGS

GREYSEXUAL

An acespec identity and umbrella term. Sexual attraction may be experienced rarely (e.g. once in a lifetime), and/or weakly (e.g. not strong enough to act on), and/or ambiguously (e.g. uncertain if sexual attraction is experienced).

ACEFLUX

An identity that fluctuates between any of the orientations in the asexual spectrum (e.g. asexual, demisexual, greysexual—including micro-labels under the greysexual umbrella).

AROSPEC ♥

The arospec flag was created to represent all identities on the aromantic spectrum. However, it's also common to see the aromantic flag (green, green, white, grey, black) representing not only the individual aromantic identity but also the entire aromantic spectrum.

AROMANTIC ♥

A romantic orientation in which the individual specifically experiences no romantic attraction. An aromantic person may experience many forms of love/attraction, though none are experienced romantically.

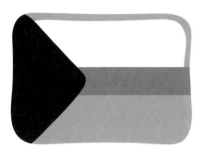

DEMIROMANTIC 🩶

An arospec identity in which romantic attraction may occur only after a strong emotional bond has formed. However, there is no set time frame in which, or guarantee that, this could happen with each partner.

GREYROMANTIC 🩶

An arospec identity and umbrella term. Romantic attraction may be experienced rarely (e.g. once in a lifetime), and/or weakly (e.g. not strong enough to act on), and/or ambiguously (e.g. uncertain if romantic attraction is experienced).

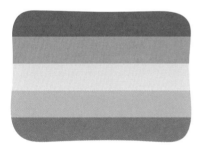

AROFLUX 🩶

An identity that fluctuates between any of the orientations in the aromantic spectrum (e.g. aromantic, demiromantic, greyromantic—including micro-labels under the greyromantic umbrella).

AROACE 🩶🩶

A combined sexual and romantic orientation in which the individual is anywhere on the aromantic spectrum *and* anywhere on the asexual spectrum (e.g. demiromantic and asexual).

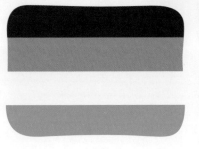

ORIENTED AROACE

An identity under the aroace umbrella in which the individual is specifically aromantic and asexual. An oriented aroace individual can experience significant forms of tertiary attraction (such as alterous, platonic, aesthetic, sensual, emotional, etc.) alongside their aromantic and asexual orientations.

Examples may include aromantic, asexual, and pan-aesthetic/sensual (panoriented aroace), or aromantic, asexual, and biqueerplatonic (bioriented aroace).

ANGLED AROACE

Under the aroace umbrella, angled aroace individuals are not strictly aromantic and asexual, experiencing significant, additional forms of romantic and/or sexual and/or tertiary attraction alongside their arospec and acespec orientations.

Examples may include aromantic and demisexual/pansexual, or aroflux/bialterous and demisexual/bisexual.

ABROSEXUAL
ABROROMANTIC

Fluid sexuality and/or romanticism, fluctuating between any number of orientations (e.g. hetero/straight, then ace, then pan, and so on).

Its Greek prefix, 'abro', means 'graceful/delicate'—possibly to reflect the flow/fragility of each shift in orientation.

PRIDE FLAGS

INTERSEX

Separate from gender identity or sexual/ romantic orientation, intersex concerns a person's classification of biological sex. Intersex people are born with characteristics that differ from traditional male or female classifications; hormones, chromosomes/genes, genitalia, or reproductive organs.

INTERGENDER ●

Though previously used by some non-intersex people, this identity has shifted towards representing some non-binary intersex people whose gender is tied to/affected by their unique and individual experience of being intersex.

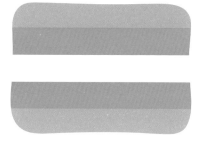

TRANSGENDER ●

Any person whose experience of gender is different to that assigned at birth falls beneath the trans umbrella. As an identity (e.g. 'trans woman'), the degree/type of social and/or physical transition will vary for each individual and is not deemed compulsory in order to identify as such.

NON-BINARY ●

Can be used as a singular identity in addition to an umbrella term. Describes any person whose experience of gender is neither exclusively 'man' or 'woman', and/or is neutral, and/or is void. This experience of gender might be static or changeable (fluid, abrupt, or overlapping).

PRIDE FLAGS

GENDERFLUID ●

An identity in which gender feels fluid, moving across the gender spectrum without a consistently fixed place, and with each experience being experienced at a mostly level/equal intensity.

GENDERFLUX ●

An identity and umbrella term in which the suffix, 'flux', means 'continuous change'. Gender fluctuates across the gender spectrum, with each experience at noticeably different intensities.

GENDERQUEER ●

An identity and a very broad umbrella term that represents a 'queering' of typical gender expression and/or presentation and/or expectations. A genderqueer person's identity can be experienced anywhere within/beyond the gender spectrum.

AUTIGENDER ●

Used by some autistic people to describe how their gender is directly affected by their individual experience of autism. Autigender people have a different connection with, or perception/experience of, gender due to their neurodivergence.

PRIDE FLAGS

DEMIGIRL ●

An identity in which a person (regardless of ASAB/AGAB) feels a strong connection to womanhood/femininity, but not enough to identify fully as a woman. Also called demigal or demiwoman.

DEMIBOY ●

An identity in which a person (regardless of ASAB/AGAB) feels a strong connection to manhood/masculinity, but not enough to identify fully as a man. Also called demiguy or demiman.

DEMINONBINARY ●

A combination of 'demi' (meaning 'half'), and 'non-binary'. An identity in which a person feels a partial connection to non-binary gender. It might be experienced as partially non-binary and partially binary, or just as partially non-binary (without any additional connection to gender).

BIGENDER ●

Two distinct genders are experienced (either alternating or simultaneously) from anywhere across the gender spectrum. For example, a bigender experience might include the genders: agender and deminonbinary.

PRIDE FLAGS

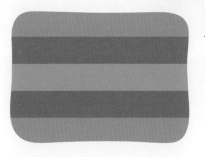

TRIGENDER ●

Three distinct genders are experienced (either alternating or simultaneously) from anywhere across the gender spectrum. For example, a trigender experience might include the genders: agender, deminonbinary, and genderfluid.

POLYGENDER ●

Multiple genders are experienced (either alternating or simultaneously) from anywhere across the gender spectrum. For example, a polygender experience might include the genders: agender, deminonbinary, genderfluid, demigirl, and woman.

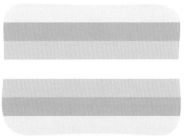

PANGENDER ●

A pangender individual experiences a sense of all genders (defined or otherwise), either alternating or simultaneously. This may also be described as experiencing gender in an all-encompassing way.

GENDERFAE/GENDERDOE ●

A fluid identity in which gender is never experienced as man/masculine. This can encompass any experience of gender that is feminine, neutral, unaligned, or genderless.

68

PRIDE FLAGS

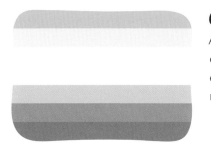

GENDERFAUN ●

A fluid identity in which gender is never experienced as woman/feminine. This can encompass any experience of gender that is masculine, neutral, unaligned, or genderless.

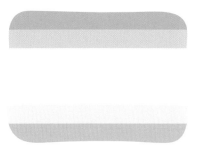

GENDERFLOR ●

A fluid identity in which gender is never experienced as man/masculine or woman/feminine. This can encompass any experience of non-binary gender (including neutral, unaligned, or genderless).

MAVERIQUE ●

An identity in which a distinct sense (beyond conventional concepts) of gender is experienced. Maverique can be described as a gender that's independent from man/masculine, woman/feminine, partially aligned, neutral, or genderless experiences.

ANDROGYNE ●

An identity and umbrella term, often described as a blend of man/masculinity and woman/femininity. This can be experienced as a combination of man/masculinity and woman/femininity, somewhere in between, or neither.

PRIDE FLAGS

NEUTROIS

Pronounced 'new-twa', this identity is used by people who *do* feel a connection with gender, although this connection is experienced as entirely neutral.

AGENDER

An identity in which a person does *not* feel a connection with gender; they may feel genderless (no gender is experienced), they may not identify with any particular gender, or they may feel removed from the concept of gender.

TWO SPIRIT

Two spirit is a complex umbrella term that usually refers to a person's gender (or 'spirit') that does not traditionally match their biology. Alongside gender roles, identity, and expression, two spirit can also include sexuality, and the sacred, spiritual, or societal roles grounded in specific beliefs/traditions of some Native American/indigenous people.

It is deemed disrespectful and inaccurate for Western/non-indigenous people to adopt the two spirit label for themselves.

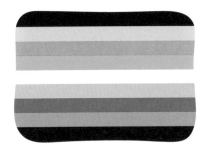

QUEER

As an identity the label can be used by individuals in which their LGBTQ+ identity feels complex or difficult to define (such as spanning multiple identity labels), or where they prefer not to specify the details of their identity—only that they are LGBTQ+. Also an umbrella term to represent all LGBTQ+ people/communities (e.g. 'the queer community', or 'a queer person').

NOTE: The term 'queer' (previously a slur) has been reclaimed by LGBTQ+ communities since the 1980s. Though 'queer' is now used to represent LGBTQ+ people/identities in a positive manner, it's important to remember that those who have experienced the term negatively may find its use uncomfortable.

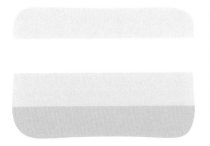

UNLABELLED

Unlabelled is an umbrella term for people who are unsure of their specific identity/orientation within LGBTQ+, those who don't wish to specifically identify as 'queer', or those who may feel restricted by any pre-existing/well-known LGBTQ+ labels.

ORIGINAL RAINBOW FLAG

Gilbert Baker created this rainbow flag in 1978 for the San Francisco Gay Freedom Day parade.

The colours represent: pink for sexuality, red for life, orange for healing, yellow for sunlight, green for nature, turquoise for magic/art, blue for serenity, and violet for spirit.

PRIDE FLAGS

RAINBOW FLAG

The most widely recognised of the rainbow flag incarnations, used to represent all LGBTQ+ people and communities. This six-stripe design was adapted from Gilbert Baker's original in 1979, removing the pink and turquoise to allow for easier manufacturing.

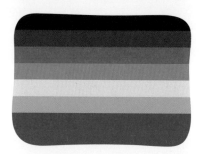

PHILADELPHIA PRIDE FLAG

In 2017, the city of Philadelphia Pride flag added brown and black stripes above the well-known six-stripe rainbow flag to recognise BIPOC (Black, indigenous, and people of colour) within the queer community.

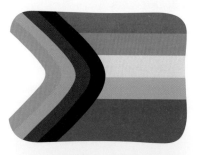

PROGRESS PRIDE FLAGS

In 2018, Daniel Quasar created the Progress Pride flag, taking the brown and black Philadelphia Pride flag stripes and adding pale blue, pale pink, and white stripes to additionally recognise trans people, non-binary people, and those living with HIV/AIDS. These colours are shaped into an arrow pointing right to symbolise the forward motion of LGBTQ+ progress.

In 2021, Valentino Vecchietti then added the intersex flag (a purple ring over yellow) within the Progress Pride flag's arrow to better represent intersex inclusion and visibility.

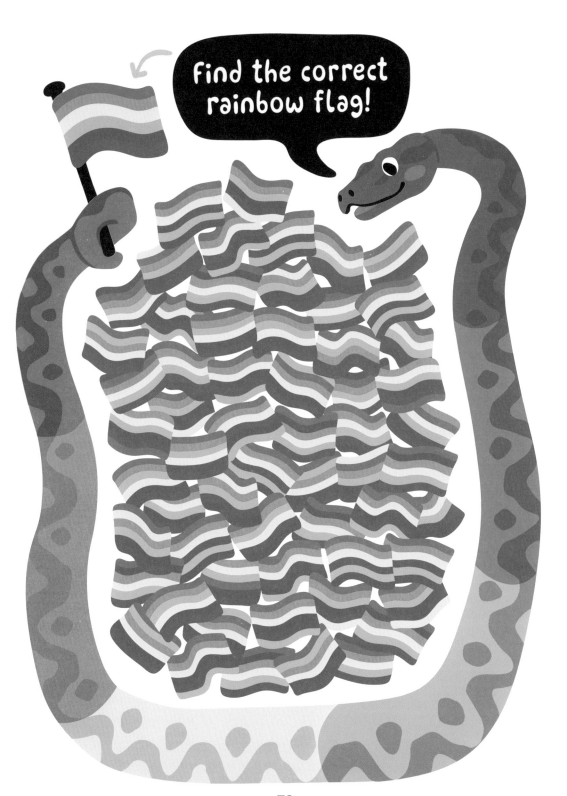

COMMON QUEER-IES

O ver time, Victoria received numerous 'queer-ies' via her social media audience surrounding queer-based topics. These ponderings and questions helped to highlight some useful areas/points that are not always covered in informative queer sources.

The list below might prove helpful with a few aspects not directly addressed within the previous sections. The original wording of those who supplied questions has been altered/generalised, with specific details (such as names or locations) being omitted to preserve anonymity.

DISCLAIMER: Any opinions or advice given are intended for informational purposes only and should not replace/substitute any advice and treatment from qualified specialists or healthcare service providers.

What doesn't the LGBTQ+ acronym/community represent?

- LGBTQ+ doesn't represent people who are heterosexual *and* heteroromantic *and* cisgender *and* dyadic (those who are not intersex).

- LGBTQ+ does not represent sexual/romantic disorders, such as attraction towards minors, inanimate objects, deceased bodies, or non-humans.

- LGBTQ+ doesn't represent non-human-based identities (e.g. otherkin or therian).

- BDSM/kink, because this is a consenting behaviour between (age-appropriate) people, regardless of having a queer or non-queer identity.

I'm struggling to figure out a specific LGBTQ+ identity, what do I do?

Identities are complex and rely on our own unique understanding and experiences to define them. Firstly, take your time. There's no pressure or deadline in which anyone needs to figure out their identity...and there's no rule to say that even once you do, that it must be applicable for the rest of your life!

Secondly, gender, sexuality, and romanticism can all be fluid, and if you find the label you've been using begins to feel less representative, then it's completely OK to find a different one that feels more representative.

Some people may never find a label that consistently describes their identity, so using broader labels like 'queer' or 'unlabelled' can help communicate inclusion under the LGBTQ+ umbrella (without needing to specify particular details).

I feel attraction to multiple genders, but I don't have the relationship experience to 'back up' my multi-sexual/romantic orientation. Am I valid?

Orientations are defined by the attraction we *feel* (how it's experienced, and the genders it's experienced towards), never the action we take in response to that. If you still feel an innate attraction to multiple genders—regardless of your relationship experience or status—you are completely valid identifying as an mspec identity.

If an allocishet person is in a relationship with a non-binary person, are they still heterosexual?

One way to view this is: an allocishet person doesn't suddenly become queer by being in a relationship with a queer person...rather, the relationship *itself* might be considered queer (such as referring to it as a 'diamoric relationship').

There really is no one-size-fits-all answer, which is why it's important to have honest, open communication surrounding pronouns and preferred terms/labels, along with the definitions all parties feel comfortable using in regard to their own personal identity and their shared relationship.

Is a heteroromantic asexual person or a heterosexual aromantic person still considered part of the LGBTQ+ community?

Neither heterosexual or heteroromantic are queer orientations. However, a person can be partly heterosexual or heteroromantic *alongside* a queer acespec or arospec identity and still be considered part of the LGBTQ+ community (because they are not entirely allosexual *and* alloromantic).

It should be noted that if an individual who is partly allo-sexual/romantic and partly ace/arospec does not feel a strong connection to queerness or the LGBTQ+ community, then they're under no obligation to consider themselves queer/LGBTQ+.

What is 'internalised homophobia'?

While the word 'phobia' *can* relate to experiencing intense fear, when added to an LGBTQ+ identity prefix (homophobia, transphobia, queerphobia, acephobia, etc.) it *actually* refers to experiencing an extreme/strong hatred or aversion to the specified identity prefix.

Phobic views can sometimes manifest internally (e.g. 'internalised homophobia') when a person denies, rejects, or suppresses their LGBTQ+ identity. A fear for one's own personal safety, along with familial or social pressures/views/treatments, can all contribute to internalised phobia. This can increase the risk of mental ill health, increase feelings of self-hatred, and stifle the ability to live freely as one's authentic self.

When should I 'come out'?

'Coming out' refers to the act of openly informing people of having an identity under the LGBTQ+ umbrella. No individual is under any obligation to 'come out' (publicly or personally), but if/when it feels comfortable to do so, ensuring the environment is safe must be a priority.

Every queer person has the right to live their own true and authentic self, free from violence, hate, or discrimination. However, it may be unsafe (particularly for some young people) to identify openly because negative LGBTQ+ views are known to be held by family members, guardians, friends, or those attending a place of education/work.

Any person facing violence, harassment, or abuse (due to their queer identity or not) should try to remove themselves—or facilitate their removal—from the situation and seek safety with trusted individuals.

I never/rarely see my specific identity in LGBTQ+ material...why is this?

When we take into account the sheer volume of (nuanced, additional, or changing) labels and micro-labels under the LGBTQ+ umbrella, there can be a tendency for LGBTQ+ educational/awareness material to focus on the broader, more commonly used identities. This might be due to specific publication/media limitations, targeting specific audiences, or even an attempt to avoid 'information overload'.

Regardless of the general public's understanding, or the quantity of exposure they receive, *all* LGBTQ+ labels and micro-labels are equally valid.

Why is 'questioning' included in the LGBTQ+ acronym?

Commonly, people who are 'questioning' feel strongly they are (in some sense) queer, but are navigating their experience and understanding of their (likely) place under the LGBTQ+ umbrella.

Questioning can be a valuable part of an individual's identity journey, and is not limited to any age, occasion, or deadline. Some queer people might feel their identity has shifted over time and they need to reassess how they identify. Others may realise they don't fit beneath the LGBTQ+ umbrella at all.

The label allows for people to feel included in queer spaces while they are exploring their identity.

I don't want to use a label. Is this wrong?

We, individually, are the only ones who can decide what label—if any at all—we want to use to help describe/communicate our identity. For many, specific labels can provide a sense of relief, understanding, and community...but, this is not true for every individual.

Some LGBTQ+ people might find labels to be restrictive or limiting and don't *want* to use them, while others might not feel *able* to connect with any specific label. If the use of a label feels wrong or uncomfortable in any way, then it's *completely fine* to not do so.

Spot ssseven differences!

SUPPORT

'Alphabet' allies

The term 'straight allies' is used for non-LGBTQ+ people who actively encourage and advocate for the rights, acceptance, and equality of minority/marginalised queer people.

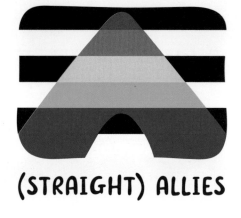

(STRAIGHT) ALLIES

Allies can play an important and integral role to help bolster LGBTQ+ support and can even use a dedicated flag (created around the late 2000s) as a tool to indicate a queer 'safe space'. An individual can also use the ally flag to show support for LGBTQ+ communities while acknowledging they, themselves, are not part of the community.

Some simple ways (for allies and queer folks alike) to support LGBTQ+ communities:

- Normalise the introduction of pronouns, for yourself and others (whether in person, or written). If you're unsure, ask what pronouns a person uses, and try to use those pronouns once they're confirmed (remember, it's OK to make mistakes when the effort/intention is sincere).

- Support and celebrate queer creators/businesses/charities.

- Be aware of LGBTQ+ current terminology/labels to avoid using any offensive/outdated terms.

- Remember, while some queer people may be happy to answer non-intrusive questions, it's not a queer person's job to teach others about their identity.

- Try to not make assumptions based on a person's appearance or gender expression.

- Discourage and challenge (where it's safe to do so) queerphobic remarks, jokes, or actions.

Outstanding organisations

It feels only right to include some of the many sources of queer information that not only proved useful in the creation of this book but are often recommended for assisting the mental and emotional wellbeing of queer people.

The type and accessibility of information/advice/support may depend on your location. Some specific services may only be available within certain countries, though many can still provide useful information or other forms of support.

NOTE: Please remember to check applicable charges before utilising any services listed below.

LGBTQ+

- The Trevor Project, www.thetrevorproject.org: The Trevor Project is the world's largest suicide prevention and crisis intervention organisation for LGBTQ+ youth. If you or someone you know needs help or support, The Trevor Project's trained crisis counsellors are available 24/7 at 1 866 488 7386, via chat at TheTrevorProject.org/Get-Help, or by texting START to 678678.

- GLAAD, www.glaad.org: An LGBTQ+ media advocacy organisation.

- LGBT Foundation, https://lgbt.foundation: A charity improving the health and wellbeing of LGBTQ+ people via skills, knowledge, and self-confidence.

- Stonewall, www.stonewall.org.uk: Campaigning as part of a global movement since 1989, helping to improve the lives of LGBTQ+ people across communities in the UK.

- Switchboard LGBTQ+ (UK) Helpline, switchboard.lgbt: Providing a safe space to inform and support LGBTQ+ people since 1974. Call: 0300 330 0630 (10am–10pm daily) or email: chris@switchboard.lgbt

- Pride in London, prideinlondon.org: Hosting the UK's biggest Pride event and raising awareness of LGBTQ+ issues, and campaigning for equality and freedom from prejudice.

- MindOut, mindout.org.uk: A service working to improve the mental health and wellbeing of LGBTQ+ people by providing online support, information, and helpline resources.

- This Is Intersex, thisisintersex.org: Information and resources regarding (and for) intersex people.

- Bi Foundation, bi.org: Providing information about bisexuality and connecting bi people around the world.

Trans and non-binary

- Trans Unite, www.transunite.co.uk: A directory resource for people in the UK searching for transgender support.

- Mermaids, mermaidsuk.org.uk: One of the UK's leading transgender and non-binary charities since 1995—supporting children, young people, and their families.

- Gendered Intelligence, genderedintelligence.co.uk: A registered charity working to improve the lives of trans and gender-diverse people. Call: 0330 355 9678 (Monday, Tuesday, Thursday 2pm–7pm and Wednesday, Friday 10am–3pm), WhatsApp chat: 07592 650 496 or email: supportline@genderedintelligence.co.uk

- Mindline Trans+, mindlinetrans.org.uk: A support helpline for emotional and mental health of transgender and non-binary people. Call: 0300 123 3393 (Monday, Wednesday, Friday 8pm–midnight).

- Gender Spectrum, www.genderspectrum.org: Providing online programmes, groups, resources, and information for young people, parents, and families.

- Life Outside the Binary, lifeoutsidethebinary.com: A safe and inclusive space for non-binary people and their allies, providing information, visibility, and support.

Acespec and arospec

- AVEN (Asexual Visibility and Education Network), www.asexuality.org: The world's largest online ace community providing an archive of resources and information on asexuality.

- AUREA (Aromantic-Spectrum Union for Recognition, Education, and Advocacy), www.aromanticism.org: A resource for aro people to enable education, awareness, and advocacy.

- Aces & Aros, acesandaros.org: A hub enabling people to get involved in their local aro and ace community.

ACTIVITY PAGE ANSWERS

NAME THE UMBRELLAS:

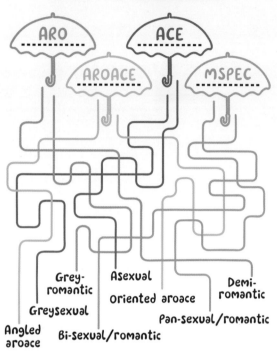

ARO

ACE

AROACE

MSPEC

Grey-romantic

Greysexual

Angled aroace

Bi-sexual/romantic

Asexual

Oriented aroace

Pan-sexual/romantic

Demi-romantic

CROSSWORD:

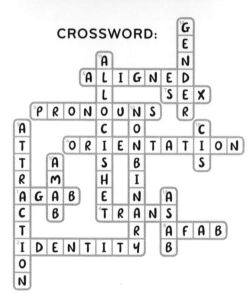

BINARY CODE MESSAGE:

T	H	E	SPACE
W	O		L
D	SPACE	R	S
SPACE	O	I	L
L	SPACE	U	F
SPACE	G	O	N
D	E	E	-
V	E	R	S
I	T	Y	

(THE WORLD IS FULL OF GENDER-VERSITY)

WORD SEARCH:

ACTIVITY
PAGE
ANSWERS

SPOT THE DIFFERENCES:

FIND THE CORRECT
RAINBOW
FLAG:

ACKNOWLEDGEMENTS

Thank you to all of the lovely people at Jessica Kingsley Publishers and Hachette who have made this publication possible. Special thanks to the JKP design team, and my wonderful editors, Andrew James (who originally suggested this guide) and Hannah Snetsinger, for enduring my many excitable ideas and queries throughout the production!

I want to also thank the people in my life who took the time to educate themselves as I explored my own identity...particularly my wonderful 'Moo-Ma', Sally, who remains one of my biggest allies.

However, the heart of this book truly lies with the LGBTQ+ community itself. Thank you for the positivity, the encouragement, and the patience, allowing me to learn from my mistakes and expand my understanding.

Thank you for the diverse voices and experiences shared—equally heart-warming as some were heart-breaking. I will be forever grateful and humbled by your support on this journey we shared; it has allowed me to continue to become a better advocate and educator...

And it's to you that this project is dedicated most of all.

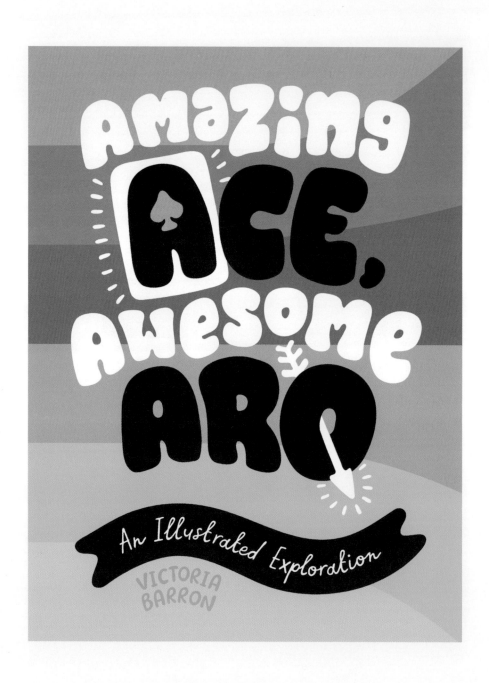